700023088X

CW01583722

LLYFRGELLOEDD BWRDEISTREF SIROL
RHONDDA-CYNON-TAF

DISCARDED
DIFETHWYD

RHONDDA-CYNON-TAFF
COUNTY BOROUGH LIBRARIES

GUNS

Theodore Rowland-Entwistle

Wayland

J623·4

Topics

The Age of the Dinosaurs
Airports
Ancient Peoples
Archaeology
Bridges
Canals
Castles
Costumes and Clothes
Earthquakes and Volcanoes
Energy
Fairs and Circuses
Farm Animals
Flags
Ghosts and the Supernatural
Great Disasters
Guns
Helicopters
Houses and Homes
Inventions
Jungles
Language and Writing
Maps and Globes
Money
Musical Instruments
The Olympics
Peoples of the World
Photography
Pollution and Conservation
Prisons and Punishment
Railways
Religions
Robots
The Seasons
Ships
Shops
Spacecraft
Stamps
Television
Trees of the World
Tunnels
Under the Ground
The World of Sharks
Zoos

RHONDDA BOROUGH LIBRARIES

All the words that appear in **bold** are explained in the glossary on page 30.

Cover *A Nicaraguan gunner trains his anti-aircraft gun skywards.*

Editor: Sophie Davies

First published in 1988 by
Wayland (Publishers) Ltd
61 Western Road, Hove
East Sussex BN3 1JD, England

© Copyright 1988 Wayland (Publishers) Ltd

British Library Cataloguing in Publication Data
Rowland-Entwistle, Theodore
Guns. – (Topics).
1. Firearms – Juvenile literature
I. Title II. Series
683′.4 TS534

ISBN 1–85210–092–3

Phototypeset by Kalligraphics Ltd, Redhill, Surrey
Printed and bound in Belgium by
Casterman s.a., Tournai

Contents

786979

The First Guns

The story of guns begins about 800 years ago with the invention of **gunpowder**. Nobody knows where it was first made, though Arabia, China, England, Germany and India all claim to have invented it.

The first guns were made in Europe in about 1320. They were shaped like a vase, with a bowl-like base and a narrow neck, and were **cast** in bronze. Later guns were made of **wrought iron** bars welded together to form a long cylinder. The cylinder was strengthened by hoops like a barrel, which is why the term 'barrel' is used for the tube of a gun.

At first guns were used in place of the huge catapults that had been used by armies since Roman times to hurl stones against the walls of castles to smash a way in. It took a long time to break solid walls in this

Early guns, looking like a cross between rifles and cannon, used by the Indian emperor Akbar at the siege of a fort in 1568.

A soldier with an arquebus, from a manual of arms published in 1607.

way, but the **cannon** could do it much more quickly.

The first kind of hand-held gun was a tube of bronze or iron about 300 mm long, lashed to a long wooden pole. Some guns were so long that the barrel had to be supported in a forked stick driven into the ground. These handguns had a variety of names, including arquebus, musket and caliver.

Early iron guns were breech-loaders. This means that the bullet or cannonball and the charge (gunpowder) were put in from the rear end (the breech), which was then closed by a door or wedge. It was difficult to make the breech airtight, so a lot of power was lost by leakage. Iron could not then be

A muzzle-loading cannon.

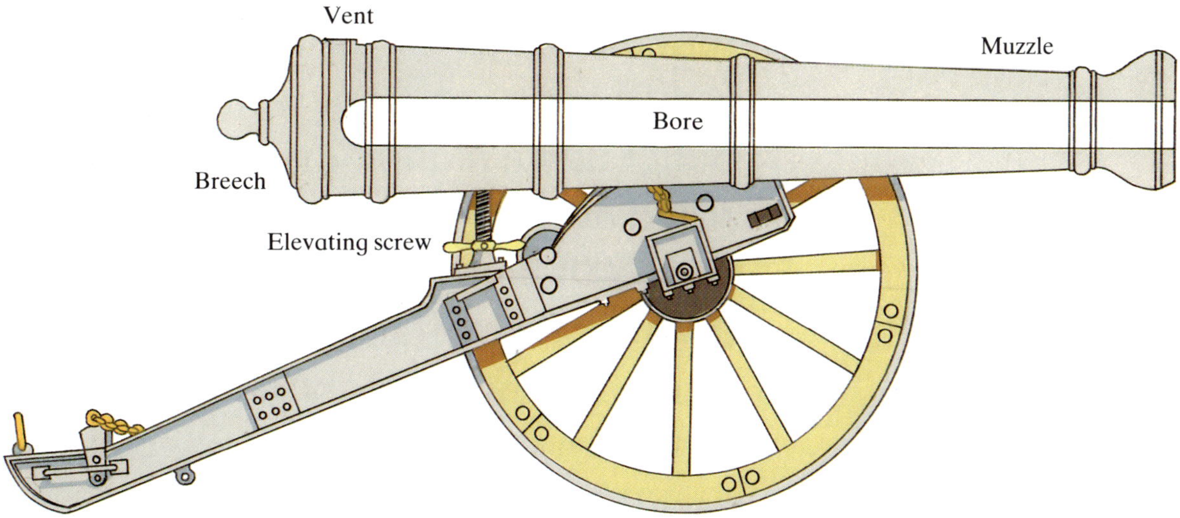

cast in large sizes, but bronze guns could be cast in one piece with a closed breech. These guns were muzzle-loaders: the charge and the cannonball were put in from the muzzle or mouth of the barrel. When iron-workers learned how to make large iron castings all guns became muzzle-loaders.

An important invention was made in the 1400s. It was **rifling**, that is, cutting spiral grooves on the inside of gun barrels. The grooves made the bullets spin, and a spinning bullet flies further and more accurately through the air. The bullet has to be slightly bigger than the inside of the barrel, and it is difficult to ram an oversized bullet down a gun barrel. However, rifled barrels came into their own in the 1800s when people discovered how to make efficient breech-loading guns. Also in the 1800s more powerful explosives such as **cordite** were invented.

Opposite *Big naval guns in close action at the Battle of Cape St Vincent in 1797.*

Big Guns

Artillery is the name given to all guns that are too large to be held in the hands for firing. Guns of all sizes are described in terms of their **calibre**, that is, the **bore** (interior width) of the barrel. It is usually given in metric measurements. Guns with a calibre of 120 mm or less are classed as light, those with a calibre between 121 and 160 mm as medium, and those over 160 mm as heavy artillery.

A giant German railway gun used during the Second World War (1939–45). Such guns could be moved about along rail tracks.

Field guns are mobile weapons that are mounted on vehicles or are towed into action. Tanks carry their own guns. A howitzer is a gun that fires high into the air so that it can hit a target behind a hill or other obstacle. A mortar is a **smooth bore** gun that can also be used against hidden targets. Unlike the howitzer it is muzzle-loaded – the soldiers simply drop a **shell** down the barrel, and it fires automatically when the shell reaches the bottom. Anti-aircraft guns fire shells high in the air to hit planes.

A 155 mm howitzer gun fitted with caterpillar tracks. It can be moved easily over rough country to attack an enemy.

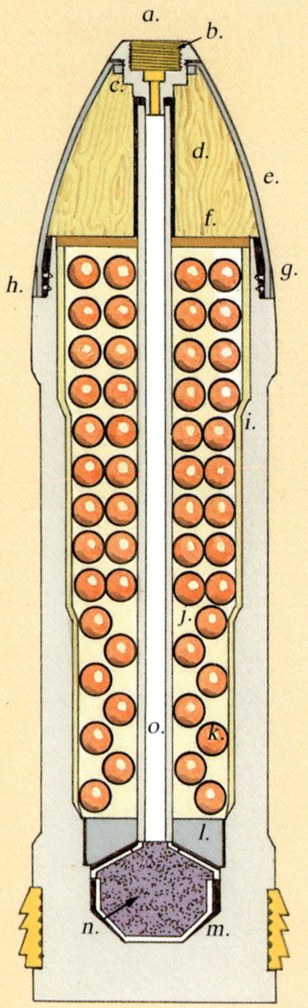

a. 2-inch (5 cm) gauge
b. Wad fuse hole 2 inch (5 cm)
c. Fuse socket
d. Wood block
e. Steel head
f. Felt wad
g. Twisting pins and rivets
h. Solder
i. Brown paper lining
j. Resin
k. 12oz (340g) steel balls
l. Steel disc
m. Tin cup
n. Bursting charge
o. Central pipe

The barrel of a modern big gun is made of steel, and is built up of several layers. The innermost layer is a huge steel bar, **forged** to the right size under giant presses. The interior is then bored out on a **lathe**.

Other tubes and hoops of steel are made, heated and fitted over the inner tube. As they cool they shrink and grip the inner tube, providing **compression** to resist the force produced when the gun is fired. Further strength is provided by winding on a layer of flat steel wire between the inner and outer tubes. When the gun barrel is finished it is rifled.

Early cannon fired cannonballs: round balls of stone or iron. Today's big guns fire shells, long pointed **projectiles** which contain **high explosives**. Some shells, known as shrapnel, are filled with metal fragments to wound or kill people.

There have been many famous big guns in history. Big Bertha was the name given to German guns which were used to shell Paris from nearly 120 km away during the First World War (1914–18). Mons Meg is a huge gun, with a calibre of 500 mm, made in 1450 and now preserved at Edinburgh Castle in Scotland. In Moscow is the Tsar Pushka (tsar cannon), a 40-tonne gun made in 1586.

Opposite *A 12-inch (30.5 cm) shrapnel shell. Shells like this were used in the Second World War.*

Below *Mons Meg, the huge fifteenth-century cannon now kept at Edinburgh Castle.*

A US Army gun crew firing a howitzer.

Hand-held Guns

Hand-held guns are known as small arms when they are used for military purposes. Handguns – **pistols** and **revolvers** – can be held and fired in one hand. Shoulder arms, such as **rifles**, are held up to the shoulder with two hands for firing. Rifles and **shotguns** are used for hunting, and rifles and pistols for target shooting. **Airguns**, which are fired by compressed air and not by an explosive, are sometimes used for sport.

Preparing to fire a rifle in target practice. The marksman wears guards to protect his ears from the effects of noise.

Troops carrying rifles in the streets of Belfast, Northern Ireland. They wear combat jackets to protect them from gunfire.

Until the early 1800s small arms were unreliable weapons. When the trigger was pressed a spark was made which set off the gunpowder, making it explode.

Modern small arms developed with the invention of the cartridge, a case that holds the **bullet**, the explosive, and a **percussion cap** or similar **detonator**, which goes off when struck and sets off the main charge. Squeezing the trigger releases a hammer which strikes the detonator.

RHONDDA BOROUGH LIBRARIES

A pistol fires one shot at a time and then has to be reloaded. A revolver is a pistol in which six or more cartridges are held in a cylinder at the breech end of the gun. When the gun is fired the cylinder revolves to bring the next cartridge into place. The first successful revolver was made by an American, Samuel Colt, in 1835.

In the automatic pistol a **magazine** or clip of cartridges is

Samuel Colt with the revolver he invented in 1835.

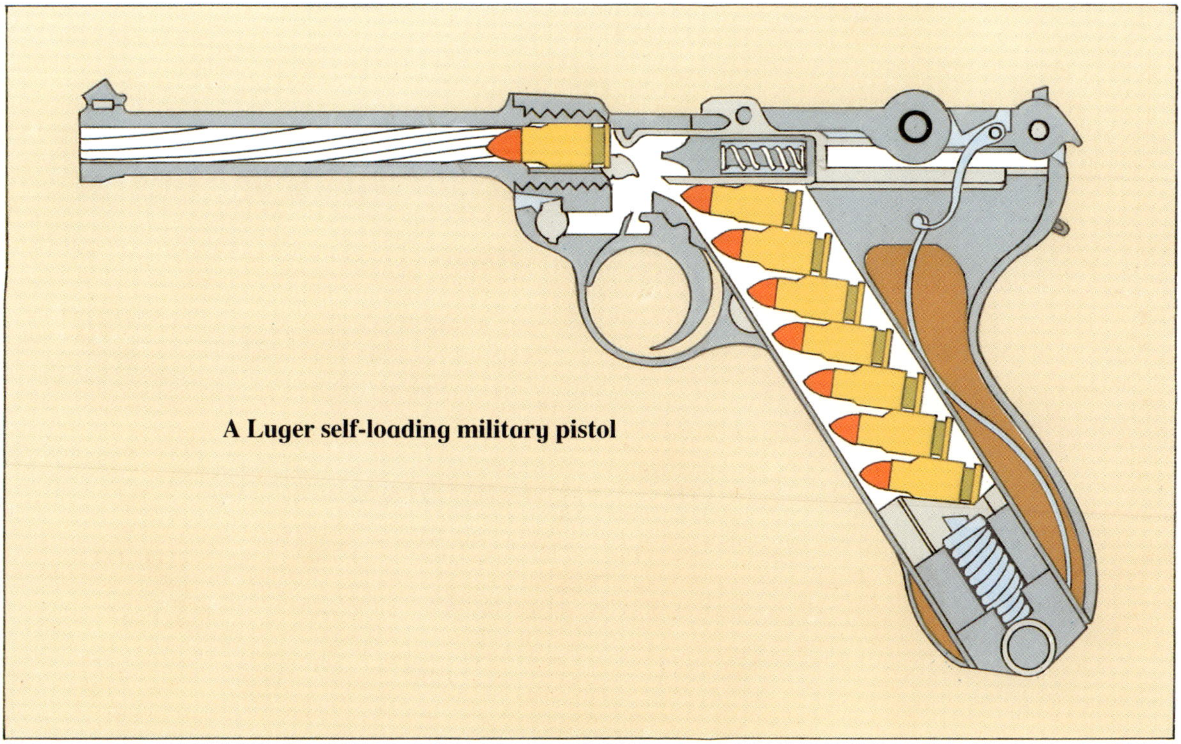

A Luger self-loading military pistol

held in the butt (handle) of the gun. As each bullet is fired a spring pushes the next cartridge up into place.

Early long-barrelled shoulder arms had smooth barrels and were muzzle-loaders. They were known as muskets. The musket used in the British Army for many years had the nickname of 'Brown Bess'. Muskets were not very accurate. Rifles are more accurate because, as the name suggests, they have rifled barrels.

A Brown Bess musket made in 1810. British soldiers used guns like this for many years.

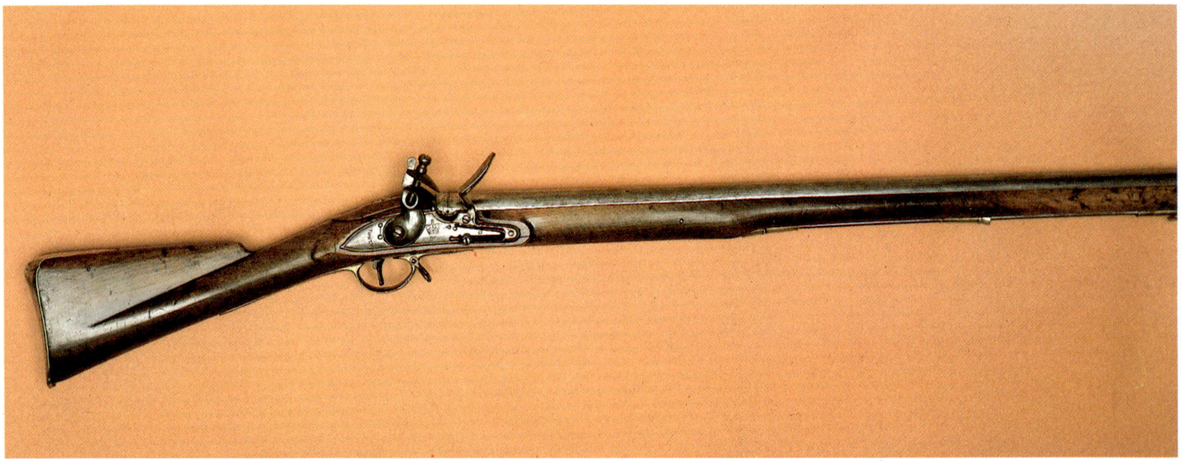

Machine guns

A **machine gun** is an automatic weapon that goes on firing as long as the trigger is squeezed. It can fire up to 1,600 bullets a minute. The **ammunition** is held either in a long belt or in a magazine.

The first successful machine gun was invented by a British engineer, James Puckle, in 1718. It was tested but never went into use. The first machine guns in battle were used in the American Civil War (1861–65), and were fired by turning a handle.

The first fully-automatic gun was made by an American-British engineer, Hiram Maxim, in 1889. His gun fired the bullet, ejected the empty cartridge case, moved the next cartridge into position, and made the gun ready to fire the next shot, all in a split second. The power for all this work came from the gun's **recoil**. Other types of

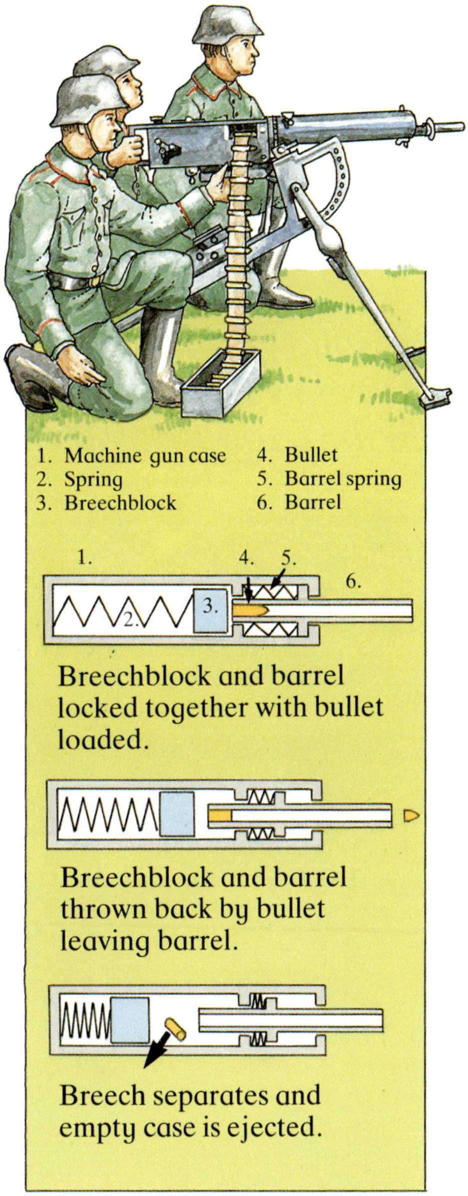

How a machine gun works.

machine gun are powered by waste gases from the explosion of the cartridge.

Machine guns played an important part in both world wars. One man with a machine gun could fight off a charge by hundreds of enemy troops. Thousands of men

Testing Hiram Maxim's machine gun in the early 1890s.

were killed in this way. Machine guns were also used in aircraft. To make aiming easier in fighter aircraft, a machine gun was mounted to fire through the whirling propeller in front of the

Machine guns like these caused terrible destruction during the First World War.

Above *A Sopwith Camel of the First World War. The machine guns fired through the propeller blades.*

Opposite *Gangsters in the 1930s used hand-held machine guns to terrorize their victims.*

pilot. The speed of firing was linked to the speed of the propeller so that the bullets did not hit the blades.

Ordinary machine guns are heavy and so have to be mounted on a support – a stand or a carriage, a tank or an aircraft. During the First World War the Germans and Italians invented a smaller machine gun that was light enough to be held in the hands. They called it a machine pistol, while the British named it a machine carbine.

Bulletin #65840 Kansas State Criminal Bureau

WANTED FOR MURDER

GEORGE KELLY alias "MACHINE GUN" KELLY

By his authority,
the Attorney General of the State
of Indiana offers a reward of

$3000.00

for information leading to the
capture of George Kelly.

DESCRIPTION

Age: 35
Height: 5-9
Weight: 185
Hair: brown
Eyes: brown
Complexion: light

CRIMINAL RECORD

Arrested Kansas City, Mo. '32, armed robbery.

Arrested Joplin, Mo. '32, attempted extortion.

Arrested Johnson City, Ka., bank holdup and shooting of law officer.

THIS MAN IS HEAVILY ARMED AND DANGEROUS. HE WAS LAST SEEN IN COMPANY WITH JOHN DILLINGER AND OTHERS OF HIS GANG.

Machine guns play an important part in modern warfare. This Royal Marine machine gun post was in action in the Falklands War in 1982.

In the United States this kind of weapon was known as a **sub-machine gun**. The most famous make was the Tommy gun, named after its designer, John T. Thompson. Later makes of sub-machine gun were the German Schmeisser, the British Sten gun, the American M3 and the Russian M41.

Guns and Society

A gun is a weapon that can kill. For this reason, governments and other authorities try to control who may or may not own guns and use them. In Britain and parts of the United States a person has to have a licence to own and use a gun.

When settlers first arrived in North America, they took guns to protect themselves against attacks, and to shoot animals for food. The **US Constitution** guarantees the right of people to carry arms. Today almost half of all American families keep a gun at home.

American citizens practise using guns for self-defence.

A Colt .45 pistol of the American West. It was used by the famous bandit Kid Curry.

A serious problem for society is the use of guns by criminals. Many robbers use guns to threaten innocent people and force them to hand over money or valuables. The growth of **terrorism** in the 1970s and 1980s has led to even more violent crimes involving the use of guns. For this reason the police of most countries carry guns, although in Britain only a few police officers are armed.

Various methods are used to combat robbers and terrorists. For example, banks and other places that are likely targets have extra-strong glass to protect their staff. They also use **closed-circuit television** to watch and record their customers.

Aircraft are particularly easy targets for terrorists. At most international airports all passengers and their luggage are examined by X-ray devices that can detect the presence of metal objects

Opposite *Armed men of the SAS (the Special Air Service) storming the Iranian Embassy in London, where terrorists held hostages in 1980.*

Armed police with dogs keep guard against terrorists at London's Heathrow Airport.

such as guns. Modern technology, however, is defeating the X-ray apparatus, because some guns are made of plastics, which do not show up on an X-ray.

Another problem of guns in society is their use in sport, such as shooting pheasants or grouse. Many people do not like the idea of shooting animals for sport.

Sporting guns, although their use is lawful, are as dangerous as any others. All guns must be handled carefully to prevent accidents. Guns should never be loaded until they are about to be used, and should never be pointed at anybody whether loaded or not.

A sportsman with a shotgun hunting wildfowl. Many people disagree with shooting animals for sport.

Glossary

Airgun Any gun which is fired by compressed air.
Ammunition Projectiles and the explosive that fires them.
Bore The interior of the barrel.
Bullet A solid projectile fired from a hand-held gun or machine gun.
Calibre The width of the bore.
Cannon A heavy gun.
Cast To shape metal by pouring it into a mould when melted.
Compression Squeezing something such as a gas into a small space.
Closed-circuit television A system in which cameras are linked in a closed circuit to television screens – usually nearby.
Cordite A cord-like explosive containing nitroglycerine.
Detonator An easily-exploded substance used to set off the main explosive in ammunition.
Forged Metal shaped by heating and hammering.
Gunpowder An explosive mixture of saltpetre, charcoal and sulphur.
High explosive Any powerful explosive such as cordite.
Lathe A machine for shaping metal or wood.
Machine gun Any light gun that fires fast repeated shots.
Magazine A case holding several cartridges.
Percussion cap A form of detonator.
Pistol A handgun with a short barrel.
Projectile Any object that can be fired from a gun.
Recoil The backward movement of a gun when it is fired.
Revolver A handgun that holds cartridges in a revolving cylinder.
Rifle A long-barrelled shoulder gun with a rifled barrel.
Rifling Spiral grooves cut on the inside of a gun barrel.
Shell A pointed projectile filled with high explosive.
Shotgun A shoulder gun that fires several small shot at a time.
Smooth bore A gun with a bore that is not rifled.
Sub-machine gun A small hand-held machine gun.
Terrorism Using violence and threats to achieve one's aim.
US Constitution The set of basic rules by which the United States are governed.
Wrought iron Iron shaped by hammering.

Books to Read

The Army by Andrew Langley (Wayland, 1986)
The Royal Marines by Theodore Rowland-Entwistle (Wayland, 1987)
The Royal Navy by Andrew Langley (Wayland, 1986)
The SAS by Theodore Rowland-Entwistle (Wayland, 1987)

Books for Older Readers
The Illustrated History of Ammunition by Ian V. Hogg (New Burlington Books, 1985)
Revolving Arms by A. W. F Taylorson (Herbert Jenkins,1967)
The Story of the Gun by Lieutenant A. W. Wilson (Royal Artillery Institute, 1976)

RHONDDA BOROUGH LIBRARIES

Picture Acknowledgements

Bridgeman Art Library 5, 9, 18; Camera Press 15, 16, 25, 28; Peter Newark's Western Americana 6, 10, 13, 17, 20, 21, 22, 23, 26; Photo Press 11, 14, 24; Rex Features *cover*; Topham Picture Library 27, 29. The illustrations on pages 7, 12, 17, 19 are by Malcolm Walker.

Index

J 623.4 R

WARFARE
WEAPONS
SOLDIERS

US 2